PORTRAIT OF NEPAL

PORTRAIT OF

NEPAL

Kevin Bubriski

Introduction by Arthur Ollman

CHRONICLE BOOKS

San Francisco

Designed by Tenazas Design, San Francisco
Printed in Hong Kong

Library of Congress Cataloging-in-Publication Data

Bubriski, Kevin.
    Portrait of Nepal / Kevin Bubriski;
    Introduction by Arthur Ollman.

        p. cm.
    ISBN 0-8118-0205-1 (hc)
        0-8118-0301-5 (pb)
    1. Nepal — Pictorial works. I. Title.
DS493.42.B83   1993
954.96 — dc20   92-14539
                                CIP

Distributed in Canada by Raincoast Books,
112 East Third Avenue, Vancouver, BC V5T 1C8

10 9 8 7 6 5 4 3 2 1

Chronicle Books
275 Fifth Street
San Francisco, CA 94103

CONTENTS

Preface

by Kevin Bubriski

IN THE MID-SEVENTIES I TRAVELED ALONE through the mountains of Nepal, living out of a backpack and relying on the hospitality of Himalayan villagers and herders for food and shelter. I spoke Nepali and found that I needed very little to live happily: a warm plate of food by a smoky fire, or space enough for my bedroll under a shepherd's rock-overhang shelter.

By the late seventies, I'd lived and worked for four years in remote Nepali villages, rarely visiting the kingdom's capital, Kathmandu. The commonplaces of modern life—cars, electricity, plumbing—had become the faint memories of another time. The rituals of mountain life were my daily reality, and my village friends and acquaintances the most important people in my life.

I was unprepared for the sense of separation I felt when I returned to the United States. Little related to the mountain villages I'd come to think of as home, and the vivid memories of my Nepal years faded as I struggled to reorient myself to modern life. Photographs were my one enduring link—like family photos in the wallet, they reminded me of those I cared for while I was far away.

In 1984 I returned to Nepal. With a view camera, tripod, sheet-film holders, a photographic assistant, and two porters, I traveled the length and breadth of the country for the better part of three years, making exposures for this book. The bulky equipment made a repetition of my earlier solo travel impossible; this time we traveled with tent, food, and cooking gear so we could live in the mountains without depleting the limited food reserves of the villagers. The static view camera set-up placed me in the midst of village life; water buffalo, goats, and curious children brushed past, occasionally bumping the tripod legs. I sometimes resented the detachment of being under the blackcloth, focused on the inverted scene on the 4 x 5 inch groundglass, rather than being fully present to the animal cries, crisp mountain breezes, and conversations around me. I was also aware of the limitations of constantly considering my hosts and their village paths and mountain vistas as visual imagery for the camera. But this second journey had its rewards.

Old friendships were rekindled and past experiences recalled as village friends from my previous stay stood before the lens. With other individuals the camera was the means of our first meeting, villager and visitor, the photographs the result of our mutual awareness. In many cases the camera recorded people who had prepared themselves and carefully presented the image of themselves they wished others to see. In other cases, the camera documented subjects with little self-consciousness or understanding of the photographic process.

Seeing the different faces—some familiar, others new, some alone, others with relatives or friends—come into focus on the groundglass, I felt I was witness to an exciting visual revelation. Upon returning to the U.S.A. and seeing the developed and printed results, I realized that I had taken a private, unique, and mysterious essence of each person out into an unknown world far beyond their mountain villages. The realization that not only my camera but also the modern world was, in turn, making ever-increasing intrusions into even the most remote areas of Nepal compelled me to document a time and a way of life slipping inexorably into the past.

Introduction

by Arthur Ollman

THE SCENE IS AN INTERIOR IN THE VILLAGE OF MANGRI above the Mugu Karnali river, where Kevin Bubriski lived for some time seven years earlier. In one of the least accessible regions of Nepal, Lama Kangri Tenzing and his young disciple face the large view camera lens of one of the only foreigners ever to visit this village. The lama stares sternly and a bit mistrustingly; the young boy's face is harder to define. This boy is expected to remain in the village and be a religious leader, and to prepare bodies of the dead for sacred sky burials, where the corpse is devoured by eagles and hawks. He sees an exotic visitor representing another world and a technology he never knew of. He, too, is recording amazing information as the shutter opens and closes. This is the beginning of his passage to knowledge of the world beyond his own village.

Several years later, Bubriski is in a different corner of Nepal setting out with a Sherpa and two unfamiliar porters. In conversation with one of the new porters, he inquires of the young man where he is from. "Mangri" is the reply. Bubriski is surprised. "Why, Mangri is in the Mugu District—that's 25 days' walk from here." This young man has clearly seen much of his country and can be considered quite worldly. The porter indicates that he has worked for Swiss mountaineers and trekkers for a few years. Bubriski relates that he, in turn, has been to Mangri, a fact that startles the porter. A curious look comes over his face and he ventures, "Kevin, is that you?"

This story is not only about chance encounters many years apart or about the intimacy of a small country sparsely populated. It is the story of all of Nepal beginning to expand its world view. As the rest of the world has come to Nepal in search of the country's beauty, harshness, solitude, simplicity, and spirituality, Nepalis have in turn been seduced out of their remote mountain villages, away from their homes, families, and tradition toward a vague dream, incompletely perceived and only partially understood. They may seek simple expansion of their perception, or material goods, or adventure. For most, the goals must be illusory and the losses great. This is by no means unique to Nepal; it may be the most common of all 20th-century tales. For better or worse, the camera is inextricably linked with it; photographs have helped lure all of us on our journeys.

For more than 500 years, one of the planet's major tragedies has been the disappearance of indigenous life forms and societies. Only in the last half of this century have the dominant cultures of the Americas, Europe, and Asia begun to realize what is being lost.

Americans are now acknowledging Native American culture as they realize the loss of an ancient interrelationship with nature. In *The Storyteller,* a 1989 novel by Peru's Mario Vargas Llosa, the protagonist argues for the survival of indigenous cultures in the late 20th century: "These cultures must be respected and the only way to respect them is not to go near them. Not touch them. Our culture is too strong, too aggressive. It devours everything it touches. They must be left alone. Haven't they amply demonstrated that they have the right to go on being what they are?" He makes his argument on behalf of the endangered Machiguenga, an Amazonian rain forest tribe.

In many places the problem affects societies too large to be seen as tribal. Nepal is a mixture of several ancient cultures, an autonomous nation, a crossroads between India, Tibet, and China for many centuries. It has already seen far too much of the modern world to ignore it, nor does it necessarily desire to do so.

We in the West tend to mourn Nepal's changes. We are conflicted about our own modernity, wanting the fruits of contemporary life, disregarding the ramifications: indigenous cultures lost, the natural world imbalanced and poisoned. Wisdom and leadership are in short supply. Our spirituality is crippled by both knowledge and doubt. We view traditional peoples as both our hope and a subject for pity. They offer ancient wisdom and solutions, yet we see them as primitives lagging far behind us. These regions of Nepal, the birthplace of Buddhism and Hinduism, are places where materialism is a dead end. Only spirituality had proven an effective balm for the harsh life. Our own ambivalence toward contemporary life echoes our split feelings about places like Nepal.

This book illuminates hard lives, barely impacted by technology. Kevin Bubriski has chosen to immerse himself and his family for years in the village life of Nepal, to explore the rich cultural, linguistic, and religious traditions and record their specificity with a classic recording device — the large view camera.

Since the early 1840s, photographers from France, England, and the United States have employed the clarity and extreme veracity of the large camera to record their impressions of tribal peoples all over the world. By the 1870s there were few areas of the globe that had not been studied through photographic "evidence" by scholars who had never been outside of Paris, London, or even New York. Governments, too, used such surveys and documentation for military and political purposes. Often photographers were the first outsiders to visit a village. The ensuing waves of visitors included armies, speculators, developers, tourists, industrialists, settlers, and intermittently more photographers. Most of these early photographers used technology nearly identical to that of Kevin Bubriski.

This curious technological displacement over more than a century reflects the rural Nepali relationship with time. The rising and setting of the sun and the seasons are far more useful than the extraneous wristwatch. Kevin Bubriski's art is not about the reflexive instantaneity of Henri Cartier-Bresson, but rather the timeless and recurring moment carefully studied. The view camera pace echoes the pace of village life, while the 35mm camera is designed for the highspeed life of places like New York, Paris, Mexico City, or Tokyo.

A 4 x 5 inch view camera with tripod is cumbersome and intrusive. It demands greater consciousness of the choices to be made and allows more time to choose. In a Nepali village the use of such equipment is something of an event in itself. The artist cannot but be a spectacle as a foreigner and photographer. Bubriski has stated that he feels in these moments that he is trying to walk through still water without making a ripple. He aspires to be a transparent technician. There is no way for him to be invisible, or even anonymous, and rapid fire sniping of images is out of the question. These formal encounters mediate the needs and expectations of both the artist and the subjects.

What comes across is not only the stark reality of beautiful but stingy land, seasons too short to produce abundant protein, and pervasive poverty, but also extraordinary respect and access. In image after image, villagers of every age stare back at us with clarity, composure, and openness. We feel their directness and try to be as open and worthy of their regard. Bubriski has placed us in this visual encounter, and, of course, it is his eyes which we are privileged to look through. Each of these people have had the opportunity to interact with his camera, and he has collected hundreds of such encounters. Kevin Bubriski is tall, far taller than most of his subjects. By lowering the camera, the subjects are seen directly, eye to eye, allowing for an equal's perspective. Never diminutized, they are shown with great dignity. The environment around them is offered to us as it appears to them. Even children are seen from the vantage point of their own peers.

The formality of this photographic interchange is due not only to slow, ponderous equipment and a formalized procedure, but also to the fact that the people are allowed the opportunity to present themselves for the photographic moment. They assemble themselves carefully for this unique experience, and by so doing illustrate their own self-respect and dignity. Bubriski understands their sense of value; he anticipates, encourages, and records it. This nourishing exchange cannot occur without trust on both sides of the lens. Bubriski's fluency goes far beyond bilingualism and the mastery of his equipment. He penetrates the marrow of this culture, understanding the history, economics, customs, beliefs, traditions, colloquialisms, and puns. Bubriski and his subjects have engaged in a moment of depiction, providing us with a window on a culture in transition. The artist knows what change may do to their delicate village subsistence. His passion is to live and work among them, recording for us this life that is still strong and vital. As Nepali village society moves away from its past, these images will offer a piece of the identity that otherwise would leach slowly from memory and tradition. Photographs have always served this function. We must be careful not to see all such imagery as mere exotica. Sensitive and respectful, these photographs will provide spiritual nourishment and generational sustenance to the Nepalis of the next century.

Five women stand on a large rock surface. Each holds a log five feet long and rhythmically lifts and pounds the log into an ancient hole in the rock. Arms moving like pistons, pounding roasted rice; the pounding has been going on here for centuries. The women come here until they are too old to do this work. Young women arrive, babies on their backs, as they came with their mothers. The children watch, the logs rise, the bodies stretch and bend, the logs drop, the old depart. Three young girls in the foreground are held steady and clear in the photograph. The movement of the pounding in the background blurs softly across the film. The arms rise, the shutter opens, the moment is recorded, the young girls stare. Those same girls today are the women pounding the rice. Their daughters now watch. The sound, the choreography, has always been with these people. This photograph might have been made 130 years ago. History and time are not linear in the village of Nira. Time is circular, repeating, and known. It is an element, like the earth, in which activities take place. Births, weddings, deaths, planting, harvest, feast, and hunger repeated. The log drops in the hole, the rice is pounded, the girl has grown old and died, as has her grandchild. The next picks up the log, as the shutter closes. Has this photograph recorded a moment or a millennium?

The Kathmandu Valley

MYTH SAYS THE KATHMANDU VALLEY WAS ONCE A LAKE surrounding the island hill Swayambhunath—the self-manifested jewel. A stroke of the Boddhisattva Manjushri's sword drained the lake, allowing humans to live on the lake floor and worship Swayambhunath. Surrounded by the foothills of the Himalayas, with the snow-peaks of the world's largest mountains arrayed along the northern horizon, the valley, twenty miles wide by thirty-five long, is a green and bountiful oasis producing crops year-round. Its several cities and towns—with their temples, shrines, carved gods and goddesses, stupas, daily religious observances, and frequent festivals—express the extraordinary spiritual and aesthetic gifts of the valley's people.

The inward, meditative attitude fostered by the valley's spiritual sites and mountain isolation is balanced somewhat by Kathmandu's role as the political and commercial hub of the country. That the place is a center of trade and cultural exchange between larger northern and southern neighbors, Tibet and India, partially explains why Buddhists and Hindus worship at the same shrines and sacred sites.

The indigenous people of the valley, the Newars, have an artistic genius and a fascination with the spiritual world that have yielded the magnificent wood-carved brick temples of Kathmandu, Patan, and Bhaktapur, intricate architectural ornamentation, and sculptures in clay, wood, silver, and gold. Their prolific artistic representations of the spiritual world complement the tantric rituals and religious festivals that dominate and order all aspects of their life. Every important event—planting, harvesting, marriage, cremation, building a house—is spiritually guided by priests, and occurs at an auspicious time chosen by astrologers.

Sacred cows—the embodiment of Laxmi the Hindu mother goddess of wealth—negotiate their way through present-day Kathmandu's traffic jams among shiny new motorcycles and cars, dilapidated Toyota taxis, diesel-spewing trucks and buses, rickshaws, cyclists, porters, and pedestrians. Global currents of change now challenge the Kathmandu Valley and its people to find a balance between the traditions of the centuries and the intrusions of the modern world.

Tukkhan Bahal, Kathmandu
1985

PLATE 2

Kwa Bahal Entryway, Patan
1987

PLATE 3

Durbar Square, Patan
1987

PLATE 4

Kwa Bahal Courtyard, Patan
1987

PLATE 5

Street Entrance to Kwa Bahal, Patan
1987

PLATE 7

Sundhara, Patan
1987

PLATE 8

Kailash Hill, Pashupatinath
1985

PLATE 10

Hanuman Ghat, Bhaktapur
1987

PLATE 11

Vishwarup Temple, Pashupatinath
1985

C H I N

2

Chu-tomu

Sa-ka

Mustang

Chi-lung
(Kyirong Dzong)

Kâgb

Tukucha

ANN

Rasua
Garhi

18450

POKHARA
VALLEY
Lamjung

Kusma

Kunchha

Nawâkot

Tanhu

Buráthum

Koch

Gurkha

Nawâkot

Babuhur

Makaising

Dhâding

Chautara

Upardáng
Garhi

Kandrang
Garhi

KATHMANDU

Narayangarhi

Bhâdgàon
Banepa

PATAN VALLEY

Trigaon

Bhikhuá Thori

Amlekhgang

Simra

Shikârpur

Bírganj

Pipra

I N D I A

The Middle Hills

THE MIDDLE HILLS LIE SANDWICHED BETWEEN THE TARAI LOWLANDS along the southern border and the icy wall of Himalayan peaks along the Nepal-Tibet border to the north. The Magar, Gurung, Limbu, and Rai villages of these Himalayan foothills are the homes of the world-famous Gurkha soldiers. Trekkers headed for Everest, the Annapurnas, Manaslu, and the other giants of the high Himalaya pass through these middle hill villages, where distances are measured not in hours or kilometers, but in numbers of days' walk.

The steep ridges and valleys that isolate one village from the next have fostered self-sufficiency. For generations, families farmed on terraces carved into the steep hillsides and lived off resources found close at hand. The land yielded timber for houses, firewood for cooking, grains for food, fodder for cattle, and cliff grasses for roofing thatch. Village blacksmiths, tailors, and shoemakers made ploughshares, clothes, plates, shoes, tools, and jewelry while village Brahmins, Lamas, or shamans tended the spiritual needs of their community.

The age-old patterns of self-sufficient isolation are now being altered by the growth of village populations and by the extension of motorable roads into communities previously reached only by footpaths. Trekking and adventure tourism in the remote villages of the middle hills have been a mixed blessing, bringing cash as well as inflation and higher material expectations to the villagers. The lure of economic opportunity draws young village men and women to Kathmandu and the large towns of the Tarai, far from the warmth of the family hearth and pastoral routines of their mountain communities.

PLATE 13

Rice Fields, Okre Village, Nuwakot
_1984_

PLATE 14
————

Tamang Couple, Gatlang Village, Rasuwa
1984

PLATE 15

Tamang Sisters, Lachang Village, Nuwakot
1984

PLATE 16

Tamang Shepherd, Doglang Village, Nuwakot
1984

PLATE 17
———

Tamang Girlfriends, Yarsa Village, Nuwakot
1984

PLATE 18

Bhairab Kund, Rasuwa
1984

PLATE 19

Tamang Father and Sons, Yarsa Village, Nuwakot
1984

PLATE 20

Tamang Brothers, Yarsa Village, Nuwakot
1984

PLATE 21

Gyamjo Lama, Haku Village, Rasuwa
1984

PLATE 22

Tamang Women, Gatlang Village, Rasuwa
1984

P L A T E   2 3

Blacksmith Sisters, Gatlang Village, Rasuwa
1984

PLATE 24

Tamang Family, Gatlang Village, Rasuwa
1984

PLATE 25

Tamang Shaman, Yarsa Village, Nuwakot
1984

PLATE 26

Gosainkund Lake, Rasuwa
1984

PLATE 27

Cornfields, Bih Village, Gorkha
1984

PLATE 28

Gurung Sisters, Labrak Village, Gorkha
1984

PLATE 29

Gurung Schoolboys, Barpak Village, Gorkha
1984

Prayer Flags, Lo Village, Gorkha
1984

Children at Bih Village, Gorkha
1984

PLATE 32

Kancha Lama, Ngyak Village, Gorkha
1984

PLATE 33

Tibetan Nuns, Sama Village, Gorkha
1984

PLATE 34

Nupri Family, Sama Village, Gorkha
1984

PLATE 36

Bih Village, Gorkha
1984

PLATE 37

Migrant Worker, Manang Village, Manang
1984

3

The Far Northwest

THE FAR NORTHWEST, NEPAL'S MOST REMOTE REGION, is blocked by four hundred miles of high mountains from the monsoon rains that sweep up from the Bay of Bengal each summer. The scant rainfall means food shortages and a cycle of hardship for the villagers of the northwest mountains.

The high-altitude Hindu villages of this region trace their ancestry to the Khasa kingdom and to a later Rajput migration from India. From the eleventh through fourteenth centuries northwest Nepal was part of the Khasa kingdom which included parts of western Tibet. Carved stone pillars and waterspouts in the Jumla, Karnali, and Sinja valleys are relics of this earlier civilization, but centuries of habitation have deforested many of the valley slopes and most of the ancient water fountains are now dry. In an effort to wring subsistence from the parched soil, even the most marginal areas are tilled for millet and barley, leaving the flat house-roofs as the only space for drying grain and holding village functions.

The Thakuri Hindus of the northwest cultivate rice at higher elevations than elsewhere in the country, and participate in trans-Himalayan trading usually practiced only by their Buddhist countrymen. The traders drive yak and sheep caravans loaded with grains into Tibet, and barter for salt, Chinese cloth, shoes, and other goods. While some of them make a good living, life for most is an endless struggle with an unyielding land. The far northwest remains a place where shamans' rituals are believed to be more powerful than modern medicines, and where suffering and fatalistic acceptance of one's *karma* is more palpable and powerful than hope.

PLATE 39

PLATE 40

Choden Tashi, Limitang Village, Humla
1985

PLATE 41

Ritual Dancers, Limitang Village, Humla
1985

PLATE 42

Mother of Thundop Lama, Dalphu Village, Mugu

1985

PLATE 43

Budhia Lama, Limitang Village, Humla
1985

PLATE 44

Konjok Lama, Kangalgaon, Humla
1985

PLATE 45

Girl with Dalai Lama Locket, Mugu Village, Mugu
1985

PLATE 46

Mugu Village, Mugu
1985

PLATE 47

Dolma, Mugu Village, Mugu
1985

Prayer Rock, Mugu Village, Mugu
1985

PLATE 49

Norbu Lama's Wife, Mugu Village, Mugu
1985

P L A T E 5 0

Buddhist Bride, Mugu Village, Mugu
1985

PLATE 51

Mugu Karnali River, Mugu Village, Mugu
_1985_

PLATE 52

Nyung Nay Retreat, Mugu Village, Mugu
1985

PLATE 53

Kama Guru, Mangri Village, Mugu
1985

PLATE 54

Chewong Chekep's Daughters, Mangri Village, Mugu
1985

PLATE 56

Kermi Village, Humla
1985

PLATE 57
_____

Blacksmith Boys, Mangri Village, Mugu
1985

PLATE 58

Dana Sheela's Family, Limitang Village, Humla
1985

PLATE 59

Newar Cousins, Jumla Bazaar, Jumla
1985

PLATE 60

Mayor's Family, Nira Village, Mugu
1985

PLATE 61

Chetri Couple, Nira Village, Mugu
1985

PLATE 62

Rara Lake, Mugu
1985

PLATE 63

Chetri Girls, Ripa Village, Humla
1985

PLATE 64

Kali Bhuda, Syara Village, Humla
1985

PLATE 65

Chetri Man and Son, Syara Village, Humla
1985

P L A T E   6 6

Servant, Nira Village, Mugu
1985

PLATE 67

Hindu Children, Karki Bada Village, Mugu
1985

PLATE 68

Hindu Shaman, Syara Village, Humla
1985

PLATE 69

Shamans' Temple, Syara Village, Humla
1985

PLATE 70

Gorha Bahadur and His Mother, Talphi Village, Jumla
1985

PLATE 71

Dan Bahadur and His Family, Syara Village, Humla
1985

4

The Tarai

THIS TEN- TO TWENTY-MILE-WIDE BAND ALONG NEPAL'S SOUTHERN BORDER marks the end of north India's vast Gangetic plain and the beginning of the Himalayan foothills. Just three decades ago the Tarai was an untamed malarial jungle roamed by tigers, rhinos, and deer. Abundant virgin hardwood forests were home to indigenous hunter-gatherer communities and later the agrarian Tharu people.

Today ninety percent of the forests are gone, the tigers and rhinos are restricted to newly established Nepali national parks and the Tarai has become the economic and industrial base of Nepal. As each monsoon washes away more of the fragile veneer of topsoil from the Himalayan slopes and terraced valleys, it is often remarked that Nepal's greatest export is free topsoil to India. Meanwhile the mountain people who have lost their land or have too little land for subsistence follow their topsoil and migrate downslope to the growing resettlement communities across the Tarai.

The region has a rich cultural heritage, being the birthplace of the Buddha and of Sita, the heroine of the Hindu epic *Ramayana*. The pilgrimage town of Janakpur in the eastern Tarai retains the flavor of the Mithali kingdom that ruled the region before the creation of modern Nepal. In the late autumn of each year Janakpur celebrates the reenactment of the wedding of Goddess Sita and Lord Rama. This love story is also expressed year-round with devotional hymns, folk songs, recitations of the *Ramayana*, and the frescoes of Ram and Sita that adorn the courtyard walls of most Mithali households. Further west in Lumbini, Tibetan, Burmese, Thai, and Japanese Buddhists make pilgrimage tours to the site of Guatama Siddhartha's birth.

In the western Tarai, legend and history tell how the Rana Tharu women fled north from India with their children and servants five centuries ago, while their men stayed behind to defend the Rajput kingdom against Muslim invasions. The Rana Tharu women settled in the forests below the Himalayas and took their servants as consorts, but they kept the upper hand in family and village affairs. Even though these hardy and assertive women still live by the traditions of their Rajput ancestors, their villages are not immune to the inroads of modernity and ecological imbalance that are changing the Tarai and all of Nepal.

PLATE 72

Rice Threshing, Arjuni Village, Kanchanpur
1986

PLATE 73

Rana Tharu Porch, Dekat Bhuli Village, Kanchanpur
1986

PLATE 74

Rana Tharu Woman, Dekat Bhuli Village, Kanchanpur
1986

PLATE 75

Rana Tharu Couple, Dekat Bhuli Village, Kanchanpur
_1986_

PLATE 77

Sita Ram's Mother, Sar Sar Village, Siraha
1985

PLATE 78

Mithali Pillar, Suga Village, Mahotari
1985

PLATE 79

Hindu Holy Men, Janaki Temple, Janakpurdham
1985

PLATE 80

Yogul Binod Kunj Ashram, Janakpurdham
1985

PLATE 81

Mithali Girls, Suga Village, Mahotari
1985

Rana Tharu Brothers, Dekat Bhuli Village, Kanchanpur
1986

PLATE 83

Bindeshwar Jha, Janaki Temple, Janakpurdham
1985

PLATE 84

Jog Ram Choudhari, Arjuni Village, Kanchanpur
1986

Captions for the Photographs

Kharanitar Village, Nuwakot 1984
Monsoon rains nourish the rice fields at the
confluence of the Dirkhu Khola and Tadi Nadie
at Kharanitar village.

Mithali Girl, Suga Village, Mahotari 1985
A young Mithali girl, Nitu Kumari, stands before
the courtyard frescoes of scenes from the *Ramayana*.
Rather than presenting a complete and accurate
depiction of Ram and Sita's wedding, the murals are
fanciful depictions that seem to be as concerned with
enlivening the walls with color and form as with
storytelling.

Lama Kangri Tenzing, Mangri Village, Mugu 1985
A young disciple, Sonam Tsering, and the Lama
Kangri Tenzing sit in the *gompa* of Mangri village
above the Mugu Karnali River. Among Kangri
Tenzing's many duties as priest is the preparation of
the corpses of the deceased for the highly meritorious
act of sky burial whereby the corpse is dismembered
atop the cliffs and fed to eagles, hawks, and vultures.

The Hulling Rock, Nira Village, Mugu 1985
On the auspicious day of the rice seed planting,
women of Nira village pound freshly roasted unhusked
rice to make beaten rice, a special celebratory treat.
Several weeks later when monsoon rains come the rice
seedlings will be transplanted into the wet terraced
paddy fields. The two months before the break of
monsoon is the critical time of food shortages and
hunger in northwest Nepal.

CHAPTER 1: THE KATHMANDU VALLEY

PLATE 1
Tukkhan Bahal, Kathmandu 1985
These Newar twin brothers have the same names
as the Hindu deity twin brothers, Ram and Laxman.
Twin sisters are usually named after the Hindu
sister river deities, Ganga and Jamuna. Although the
brothers' names are Hindu, Buddhist *stupas* and
caitya fill the courtyard of their home at
Tukkhan Bahal.

PLATE 2
Kwa Bahal Entryway, Patan 1987
The entryway *torana* at Patan's Kwa Bahal, the
Golden Temple, is one of the finest works of Newar
repoussé craftsmanship in the Kathmandu Valley.

PLATE 3
Durbar Square, Patan 1987
At dawn on a winter morning the sweepers at the
Patan Durbar Square are dwarfed by the the Krishna
temple's Garuda guardian on top of his stone pillar.

PLATE 4
Kwa Bahal Courtyard, Patan 1987
Kwa Bahal, the golden Temple, has the largest
Newar Buddhist congregation or *sangha* of all of
Patan's numerous *bahals* and *viharas*.

PLATE 5
Street Entrance to Kwa Bahal, Patan 1987
The stone sculpted façade at the entrance of the
Golden Temple hints of the extensive representation
of deities within the spacious but intimate interior
spaces of the temple.

PLATE 6
Mirghasthali, Pashupatinath 1985
The sacred forest of Mirghasthali lies above
Kathmandu's main Shiva shrine of Pashupatinath.
Mythically the abode of deer herds and the place
of Shiva and Parvati's romantic encounters,
Mirghasthali is now the home of the Goraknath
ashram and numerous *sanyasi* Shiva worshippers.

PLATE 7
Sundhara, Patan 1987
Water has flowed for centuries from the medieval
stone and brass *repoussé* fountain of Sundhara, the
"golden fountain" of Patan.

PLATE 8
Kailash Hill, Pashupatinath 1985
Hindu civil servant Guna Prasad Pundshahni
performs his daily morning worship of the great
Shiva *lingam* at Kailash hill on the grounds of
Pashupatinath temple before going to work at the
government office of publications and letters.

PLATE 9
Ee Bahal, Patan 1987
Children on their way home from school stand amid
the half constructed concrete carpet factory at the
site of the ancient Buddhist monastery of Ee Bahal.

PLATE 10
Hanuman Ghat, Bhaktapur 1987
At Bhaktapur's cremation grounds of Hanuman Ghat
a Newar man stands before the larger-than-life-size
stone image of Ganesh, the god of good fortune and
luck and the remover of obstacles.

PLATE 11
Vishwarup Temple, Pashupatinath 1985
Gopal Mun Shresta and his son Raj Kumar live
as squatters at the Vishwarup Temple in the
Mirghasthali forest on the grounds of Pashupatinath,
Nepal's most revered Shiva shrine.

PLATE 12
Swayambhunath Caityas 1987
Winter morning fog shrouds the *caityas* along the
pilgrimage route that climbs the *stupa* crowned
hill of Swayambhunath, the self-manifested jewel,
so described in the creation myth of the
Kathmandu Valley.

CHAPTER 2: THE MIDDLE HILLS

PLATE 13
Rice Fields, Okre Village, Nuwakot 1984
Newly planted terraces of paddy rice turn the village
of Okre into a patchwork of the sky's reflections.

PLATE 14
Tamang Couple, Gatlang Village, Rasuwa 1984
The postal runner Tsering Dorje Tamang of Gatlang
village poses with his flashlight and umbrella, and his
new bride, Dev Kumari.

PLATE 15
Tamang Sisters, Lachang Village, Nuwakot 1984
Sisters Kanchi and Thuli Tamang of Lachang village
sit ready with their sickles to cut loads of fodder for
the family's cattle. The family has enough food from
its own fields for only half of the year and must work
in the fields of larger landowners for food the rest
of the year.

PLATE 16
Tamang Shepherd, Doglang Village, Nuwakot 1984
Shepherd Syarki Tamang returns from the high
pasture with a sheep too weak to walk with the herd.

PLATE 17
Tamang Girlfriends, Yarsa Village, Nuwakot 1984
Girlfriends Sarki Lama and Syarki Tamang, fourteen
and thirteen years old, embrace for warmth on a damp
monsoon morning.

PLATE 18
Bhairab Kund, Rasuwa 1984
When one looks down to Bhairab Kund from the
banks of Gosainkund Lake, it is easy to understand
why devout Hindus of the region believe these two
lakes and the higher lake of Surjya Kund were created
by the thrust of Shiva's trident.

PLATE 19
Tamang Father and Sons, Yarsa Village, Nuwakot 1984
Yousinge Lobsang Tamang, aged forty-two, stands
proudly with his three sons, Dawa, Suku, and Pasang
Tsering. Among orthodox Hindus of Nepal, sons are
preferred over daughters for carrying on the family
name and worshiping the family ancestors. The
Tamangs and other hill people have accepted this
attitude to some extent.

PLATE 20
Tamang Brothers, Yarsa Village, Nuwakot 1984
Brothers Barcha Bahadur and Sukla Tamang sit
before woven bamboo mats which are used as
containers for the harvests as well as roofs for
shepherds' shelters.

PLATE 21
Gyamjo Lama, Haku Village, Rasuwa 1984
Gyamjo Lama is the principal Buddhist priest of
his Tamang village of Haku. Here he returns with
fodder for his cattle early one monsoon evening.

PLATE 22
Tamang Women, Gatlang Village, Rasuwa 1984
Pasang Tamangni and Kami Tamangni have shared
decades of daily chores together as neighborhood
friends and as two of the oldest villagers of Gatlang.

PLATE 23
Blacksmith Sisters, Gatlang Village, Rasuwa 1984
Sisters Dil Mia, fifteen years old, and Myli Chundi,
thirteen years old, of the blacksmith caste, wear
the finest blouses and skirts owned by the family.
The stigma of untouchable caste is very much part of
the lives of families of the blacksmiths, shoemakers,
and tailors of Nepal. The blacksmith families
of Gatlang village form one extended family that
originally migrated from Dhading District seven
generations ago. They are all landless and earn their
livelihood from bartering and selling their
ironsmithed wares of tools, *khukris*, pots, and pans.

PLATE 24
Tamang Family, Gatlang Village, Rasuwa 1984
Sitar Tamang is the neighborhood representative
to the village development committee and is forty-
three years old. Here he stands with his wife
Chengwa and daughter Gurungsia before their rough
plank–roofed house in Gatlang village.

PLATE 25
Tamang Shaman, Yarsa Village, Nuwakot 1984
Shaman Shing Tchor Tamang displays his shaman
bells and drum outside of his home, a dwelling for
his family as well as his workplace for healing and
performing exorcisms.

PLATE 26
Gosainkund Lake, Rasuwa 1984
The sacred lake of Gosainkund clears from under
monsoon fog to reveal a sunlit reflection of the far
shore. The mid-monsoon festival of *Janai Purnima*
brings hundreds of Hindu and Buddhist pilgrims to
the lake for spiritual renewal.

PLATE 27
Cornfields, Bih Village, Gorkha 1984
The cornfields of Bih village grow above the narrow
and steep Buri Gandaki River gorge at the beginning
of the Nupri Valley.

PLATE 28
Gurung Sisters, Labrak Village, Gorkha 1984
These Gurung sisters of Labrak village each have
sons serving in the Indian army. Like the Gurungs
of neighboring Barpak village, many of the
young Gurung men of Gorkha and other middle
hill districts join the British or Indian armies as
conscripts.

PLATE 29
Gurung Schoolboys, Barpak Village, Gorkha 1984
These Gurung schoolboys of Barpak village are the
sons of Gurkha British army veterans.

PLATE 30
Prayer Flags, Lo Village, Gorkha 1984
Prayer flags herald the Buddhist monastery of Lo
village in the Nupri Valley. The people of the Nupri
Valley are Nepali citizens, yet they practice Tibetan
Buddhism and are active trans-Himalayan traders
who make frequent trips into Tibet.

PLATE 31
Children at Bih Village, Gorkha 1984
These young boys and girls of Bih are more likely
to speak the local Tibetan dialect rather than the
Nepali language of their Hindu Gurung neighbors
who are three days' walk south down the Buri
Gandaki River gorge.

PLATE 32
Kancha Lama, Ngyak Village, Gorkha 1984
Kancha Lama of Ngyak village is a spiritual leader in
his village as well as a veteran high altitude porter for
expeditions to the neighboring Himalayan peak of
Manaslu. From his house he overlooks the
confluence that drains the Nupri Valley to the west
and the Tsum Valley to the east.

PLATE 33
Tibetan Nuns, Sama Village, Gorkha 1984
At Sama, the largest village of the Nupri Valley,
there are monastic communities of Tibetan Buddhist
men and women.

PLATE 34
Nupri Family, Sama Village, Gorkha 1984
A Tibetan man of Sama sits with his daughter and
very young son.

PLATE 35
Lama of Prok, Lo Village, Gorkha 1984
The reincarnate Lama of Prok, Tulku Tay Gyamtso,
is flanked by two of his monk attendants during a
recess in his delivery of Tibetan Buddhist teachings at
the monastery in Lo village.

PLATE 36
Bih Village, Gorkha 1984
This young girl of Bih village stands by a basket
holding part of the household's barley harvest.

PLATE 37
Migrant Worker, Manang Village, Manang 1984
This migrant worker is a Newar from Kathmandu
hired by the wealthy landowners of Manang village
to bring in the barley harvest. Many Manang people
have left their village north of Annapurna to live
comfortably in Kathmandu on the money they have
made trading in Hong Kong, Bangkok, and
Singapore.

PLATE 38
Women of Manang Village, Manang 1984
The women outnumber the men present in Manang
village. While the women tend to the elderly,
children, and infants, the men are frequently away
on trade and business ventures.

PLATE 39
Limitang Village, Humla 1985
The flat-roofed houses of Limitang village perch high above the Dozam Khola, in the last permanent settlement before Rawling Gompa and the trail across alpine pastures and snowy passes into Tibet.

PLATE 40
Choden Tashi, Limitang Village, Humla 1985
Choden Tashi and his daughters live in Limitang village of northern Humla. He is a trans-Himalayan trader and like most of the men in the village has studied the Tibetan Buddhist tradition.

PLATE 41
Ritual Dancers, Limitang Village, Humla 1985
In Limitang the ritual movement of masked and costumed village men reenacts the passage of the spirits of deceased beings into the next life.

PLATE 42
Mother of Thundop Lama, Dalphu Village, Mugu 1985
The mother of trader and yak herder Thundop Lama has been blind for over two decades. In the rough terrain of Dalphu village it is rare for her to ever leave the family hearth where she routinely grinds the grain for the family on the heavy stone hand-driven mill. When not by the hearth she maintains her perch on the plank bench outside the door of the house.

PLATE 43
Budhia Lama, Limitang Village, Humla 1985
Budhia Lama of Limitang holds little land of his own and usually works for the families with large herds and land ownings. With sheepskin robe and *bakpa* ritual mask his dance reenacts the deceased's journey into the next life.

PLATE 44
Konjok Lama, Kangalgaon, Humla 1985
Konjok Lama and his son Pema Yeshe stand before the wall of their monastery home. The son is now learning the Tibetan scriptures and Buddhist practice from his father, who is the spiritual leader of the village.

PLATE 45
Girl with Dalai Lama Locket, Mugu Village, Mugu 1985
The people of Mugu village are devout followers of Tibetan Buddhism and the Dalai Lama. They often combine trade and spiritual pilgrimage on trips to Mt. Kailash in Tibet and to Boudhanath *Stupa* Kathmandu.

PLATE 46
Mugu Village, Mugu 1985
Most salt for the middle hills region of Nepal now comes up from the Indian border due to the impact of the Chinese occupation of Tibet on trans-Himalayan trade and the arrival of motor roads from Nepal's southern border. The diminished salt trade with Tibet means that the adjoining houses of Mugu village are often vacant.

PLATE 47
Dolma, Mugu Village, Mugu 1985
Dolma and her family spend the summer season in Mugu village and the winter season in the Mugu District government headquarters where she sells her distilled rice wine and fermented millet beer to the civil servants. Here she hulls millet grain before grinding it by hand into flour for breads and porridge. Her large hoop earrings are unique to the Buddhist women of the Mugu Karnali Valley.

PLATE 48
Prayer Rock, Mugu Village, Mugu 1985
At thirteen thousand feet altitude, rocks carved with prayers adorn the otherwise austere landscape of Mugu village. Buddhists of the Himalayan region believe that the building of *stupas* and *chortens*, often cairn-like piles of rough or prayer-carved rocks, gives merit to the builder as well as guidance to pilgrims along the trail.

PLATE 49
Norbu Lama's Wife, Mugu Village, Mugu 1985
Norbu Lama's wife bundles herself in her black wool Mugu blanket. She and her husband live in quiet, solitary retreat away from the village.

PLATE 50
Buddhist Bride, Mugu Village, Mugu 1985
The day after her wedding the bride wears the lockets of bundled prayers on paper that she received from the officiating Lama.

PLATE 51
Mugu Karnali River, Mugu Village, Mugu 1985
This young boy sits by the monsoon-swollen Mugu Karnali river whose headwaters are a couple of days' walk north in Tibet. Behind the boy is Mugu village and the waterfall along which runs the footpath east to Dolpo district.

PLATE 52
Nyung Nay Retreat, Mugu Village, Mugu 1985
Norbu Lama, Chuba Lama, and Sheynang Lama have undertaken a three-day fast and retreat of silence *nyung nay* in order to reap spiritual merit. The three days are spent in a tent on the spacious grassy riverbank an hour upstream from the din of village.

PLATE 53
Karma Guru, Mangri Village, Mugu 1985
Karma Guru is one of the village committee representatives of Mangri. Here he stands with the two youngest of his four sons. In 1987 his oldest son was one of the first two high school graduates of Mangri village. Seven years earlier the village schoolteacher had only a fourth grade education; Mangri now boasts its own high school with new graduates each year.

PLATE 54
Chewong Chekep's Daughters, Mangri Village, Mugu 1985
Paljom and Dawa Dolma are the two surviving daughters among Chewong Chekep's four children. His father and other two daughters all passed away in the same spring season. In Mangri village and in most villages of the Karnali Zone the infant mortality rates are the highest in Nepal, reaching up to seventy percent.

PLATE 55
Yablang, Mugu 1985
High above the confluence of the Mugu Karnali River coming from the Tibetan border and the Langu River coming out of northern Dolpo sits the seventeen-thousand-foot altitude pilgrimage destination of Yablang. Yablang is the most revered site of the Mugu region as evidenced by the hundreds of slate *chortens*, memorial monuments erected by Buddhist pilgrims. Equally respected and revered by Hindus who call the sacred site Chayanath, it is the focal destination for their monsoon pilgrimage at *Janai Purnima*.

PLATE 56
Kermi Village, Humla 1985
Kermi village is the last sizeable year-round village on the Humla Karnali river route to Mt. Kailash in Tibet. Though it is a Buddhist village it is frequently visited by the Hindus of the northwest on trade trips into Tibet or on the pilgrimage route to Mt. Kailash, the abode of their Lord Shiva.

PLATE 57
Blacksmith Boys, Mangri Village, Mugu 1985
Two blacksmith boys have been sent by their landless families to search for food in Mangri village after the winter wheat and barley harvest. The hungry may be given grain by compassionate villagers. More commonly grain is bartered for the blacksmiths' services or for their labor in the fields of the landowners. Grain or money is borrowed at the rate of five percent a month which starts an endless spiral of indebtedness to the landowners.

PLATE 58
Dana Sheela's Family, Limitang Village, Humla 1985
Dana Sheela and her parents stand before the front door of the small house given to them by a wealthy landowning trader family in Limitang village. Her family subsists on food bartered for her father's smithing work and by their shared labor in the landowners' fields.

PLATE 59
Newar Cousins, Jumla Bazaar, Jumla 1985
These first cousins are sons of Newar merchants in Jumla Bazaar, the government administrative seat for the Karnali Zone. Their families have lived for the past full generation in Jumla and travel at least once a year by airplane to Kathmandu.

PLATE 60
Mayor's Family, Nira Village, Mugu 1985
The jewelry and garments of these two women of Nira village in Mugu district recall the Rajput ancestry of the high caste Hindu Thakuri people of northwest Nepal. Locally woven yak wool blankets provide the backdrop for the mayor's wife, daughter-in-law, and grandchildren.

PLATE 61
Chetri Couple, Nira Village, Mugu 1985
A yak wool blanket draped over stacks of baskets forms a backdrop for this Hindu Chetri couple who have no surviving children. Behind them are their neighbors on the communal front porch in Nira.

PLATE 62
Rara Lake, Mugu 1985
Rara Lake rests at ten thousand feet altitude in the center of Mugu District. Originally the two Hindu villages of Rara and Chapru sat above the lake's northern shore. When Rara Lake was established as a National Park in 1978 all the inhabitants of the two villages were forced to relocate nine days' walk south to the nearly sea-level land in the Tarai.

PLATE 63
Chetri Girls, Ripa Village, Humla 1985
The Hindu Chetri girls Yangi Matara and Chauta Matara stand before a backdrop of Ripa village's beehive styled architecture high above the Humla Karnali River.

PLATE 64
Kali Bhuda, Syara Village, Humla 1985
Kali Bhuda and his brother both suffer from thyroid iodine deficiency common in northwest Nepal. He lives with his family in Syara village and contributes his labor to the chores in the fields, hauling water from the nearby tap and gathering firewood.

PLATE 65
Chetri Man and Son, Syara Village, Humla 1985
A Chetri man and his son stand at the doorway of their home in Syara village.

PLATE 66
Servant, Nira Village, Mugu 1985
This orphaned boy of the untouchable tailor caste is a servant for one of the wealthier Thakuri families of Nira village.

PLATE 67
Hindu Children, Karki Bada Village, Mugu 1985
While all of the women are at work in the fields the young girls stay behind on the rooftops with their younger siblings. At a very early age the Thakuri and Chetri girls of Karki Bada village also learn the routines of laboring in the fields, herding the cattle, and hauling water and firewood.

PLATE 68
Hindu Shaman, Syara Village, Humla 1985
This Hindu shaman of Syara village in Humla has not cut his silver banded locks since his initiation several decades ago. Hindu shamans of Humla usually make the pilgrimage to Manasaraovar in Tibet for sacred baths of ablution which cleanse them for their duties as spiritual mediums.

PLATE 69
Shamans' Temple, Syara Village, Humla 1985
A shepherd and two village boys from Syara stand before the shamans' temple in the jungle above the village. The large bell and drum are used to awaken and call the spirit to the shaman. Only the shamans are allowed into the temple; in the remote villages of Humla and throughout Nepal they help mark rites of passage, exorcise the evil spirits that bring illness, celebrate the phases of the moon, and bring rain at times of drought.

PLATE 70
Gorha Bahadur and His Mother, Talphi Village, Jumla 1985
Two-year-old Gorha Bahadur sleeps on his mother's back at Talphi village on the Chautabise River a day's walk east of Jumla Bazaar. The Chetri Hindus of the Chautabise Valley are less strict about the prohibition against drinking. A variety of corn-, millet-, and rice-fermented beer are made in their villages. The Chautabise Valley runs parallel to the Mugu Karnali Valley, though they are separated by an eighteen-thousand-foot pass and four-day walk. The Chautabise Valley is the winter grazing ground for the yak herds of the Mugu villagers, and many of the people have built homes and resettled on the Chautabise, creating their own village at Matichaur.

PLATE 71
Dan Bahadur and His Family, Syara Village, Humla 1985
Although Dan Bahadur Nepali is a proud veteran of the Indian army, in his village of Syara in Humla he and his family are regarded first and foremost as untouchables of the blacksmith caste. His worldliness is most conspicuously expressed by his ownership of the largest radio in the village. He is more literate and aware of the outside world than most of his fellow villagers, though many of them are trans-Himalayan traders who bring their herds of sheep from the snowy Tibetan plateau to the sweltering inner Tarai valley of Surkhet to the south.

PLATE 72
Rice Threshing, Arjuni Village, Kanchanpur 1986
A bountiful harvest of paddy rice is threshed by the cattle's hoofs in Arjuni village of Kanchanpur. In 1989 Arjuni village was razed and its fifty families relocated to make room for the enlargement of Sukla Phanta National Park. Four hundred and fifty households of other villages were also relocated.

PLATE 73
Rana Tharu Porch, Dekat Bhuli Village, Kanchanpur 1986
The spacious porches of Rana Tharu households are a place for grain storage and for cool refuge from the sun's heat in the sea-level Tarai. The Rana Tharu porch usually has separate fires for the men and women. Compared to other caste groups throughout the Tarai and Nepal, the Rana Tharu women have a more powerful and autonomous role in the household and in the village.

PLATE 74
Rana Tharu Woman, Dekat Bhuli Village, Kanchanpur 1986
Like a breastplate of armor, silver vests made from rupee coins are part of everyday jewelry of the Rana Tharu women. A woman's brass anklets, also worn daily, can weigh up to three pounds on each leg. The loose short skirt and jewelry of the Rana Tharu women encourage them to strut proudly in large steps rather than move with the small restricted steps determined by the *sari* worn by most Nepali women.

PLATE 75
Rana Tharu Couple, Dekat Bhuli Village, Kanchanpur 1986
This newlywed Rana Tharu couple in Kanchanpur show the persistence of Rana Tharu tradition in the wife's body ornaments, compared to the wristwatch and generic tee shirt of the husband.

PLATE 76
Dangora Tharu Family, Arjuni Village, Kanchanpur 1986
Dangora Tharu grandparents in Arjuni village pose with some of their grandchildren. Dangora Tharus are different from the Rana Tharus in that they migrated to Kanchanpur not from Rajput India but from the Dang Valley in Nepal's Tarai, several days' walk east of Kanchanpur. Dangora Tharu households can number up to forty or fifty people in the extended family of grandparents, their siblings, all their sons, and their sons' families.

PLATE 77
Sita Ram's Mother, Sar Sar Village, Siraha 1985
In the eastern Tarai of Siraha this woman smokes tobacco in her homemade coconut seed water pipe. In the village of Sar Sar her son Sita Ram has four children, a college degree, and past careers as school teacher and the village mayor. He is now a Hindu holy man of the Vaishnav sect.

PLATE 78
Mithali Pillar, Suga Village, Mahotari 1985
Like a lone sentry guarding the house this sculpted column of wood and clay expresses the interrelation of artistic expression with daily life in the Mithali villages of the eastern Tarai. Before establishment of the Nepal-Indian border by the British, the Mithali kingdom extended from the Himalaya into the Gangetic plains west of Calcutta. Even today Mithali marriages are frequently between families living across the border from each other. Essential to Mithali marriage is the creation of frescoes on the courtyard walls of the house and the specially designated wedding room. The frescoes portray scenes or figures from the *Ramayana*, the epic of Ram and Sita's love, and figures of fertility.

PLATE 79
Hindu Holy Men, Janaki Temple, Janakpurdham 1985
These three Hindu holy men are worshipers at the Janaki Temple in Janakpurdham. Janak, the father of Sita the heroine of the *Ramayana*, is worshiped in Janakpur along with his daughter and son-in-law Ram. Every year, a reenactment of the marriage of Ram and Sita attracts several thousand Hindu pilgrims from Nepal's hills and Tarai and from across the Indian border. On the outskirts of the town are numerous bathing ponds and *ashrams* for holy men and women and pilgrims.

PLATE 80
Yogul Binod Kunj Ashram, Janakpurdham 1985
At Yogul Binod Kunj Ashram, four young attendants take care of cleaning, bringing wood and water, and other daily tasks dictated to them by the *mahant* leader of the Hindu monastic place of retreat.

PLATE 81
Mithali Girls, Suga Village, Mahotari 1985
In the heat and extreme humidity of the monsoon in the Tarai these young Mithali girls take a break from chores in the household courtyard.

PLATE 82
Rana Tharu Brothers, Dekat Bhuli Village, Kanchanpur 1986
Two Rana Tharu brothers with sunglasses emulate the King of Nepal in the poster behind them.

PLATE 83
Bindeshwar Jha, Janaki Temple, Janakpurdham 1985
Bindeshwar Jha is a Mithali high caste Brahmin and is one of a handful of *pujari* caretakers at the Janaki Temple. His two most essential duties are the performance with the other *pujaris* of the morning and evening worship to the idols of Ram and Sita in the temple's central chamber. The morning *puja* and the evening *arati* attract numerous worshipers with the loud clanging of cymbals and bells, the showering of Ram and Sita with holy water and flower petals, the singing of devotional music, and finally the blessing of all who have come for worship.

PLATE 84
Jog Ram Choudhari, Arjuni Village, Kanchanpur 1986
Jog Ram Choudhari was the governor of Kanchanpur District and a supporter of the King of Nepal, whose portraits he holds in front of him. One of his many grandsons stands at his side. Jog Ram was the leader of Arjuni village, which in 1989 was leveled by the government's enlargement of the Sukla Phanta National Park. The park represents a victory for the wildlife of the Kanchanpur area, but this grandson will never have the chance to work the land and live from the harvests that are his birthright.

CAPTIONS FOR THE PHOTOGRAPHS
The Mugu Karnali River at Mugu Village, Mugu 1985
Monsoon fog engulfs the Mugu Karnali River valley at Mugu Village. The stone hut across the river serves as shelter for the Hindu traders who come up from the lower Mugu Karnali and Sinja River valleys to trade their grain for salt that the Mugu villagers bring down from Tibet.

Acknowledgments

I am grateful to the people of Nepal who have taught me about their homeland and who have given me guidance in my years in Nepal. I especially wish to thank all the individuals who patiently stood or sat before the camera, those who appear here as well as the many who do not. I thank His Majesty's Government of Nepal and the American Peace Corps Nepal for introducing me to Nepal, its people, and its language.

Norkay Sherpa was invaluable as my assistant in 1984 and 1985 for seven months of fieldwork in the middle hills and northwest region of Nepal. I am grateful to Keshar Shahi and Dhan Bahadur Shahi of Karki Bada, Mugu District, and Setok Lama and Wangchu Lama of Mangri, Mugu District, for their labors as porters throughout the Karnali Zone in the springtime season of hunger. Chewong Chekep Lama of Mangri, Kamishwar Pandey of Suga, Chandra Singh of Kanchanpur, Tenzing So Sher of Lo, Bharat Jung Upreti of Kharanitar, and their families are but a few of the numerous hosts who generously offered their warm hospitality.

Judith Chase, Charles Gay, Pam Ross, and Ted Wooster, living in Nepal, were helpful and appreciative throughout the duration of this work. I remember my late friend Hugh Swift whose insistent encouragement brought me back to Nepal in 1984. Robert Gardner and the Film Study Center of Harvard University were especially supportive of my photographic work in Nepal. Brad Bealmear, John Gruen, John McKee, Abelardo Morell, Walter Nelson, William Pierson, Ada Takahashi, and Clark Worswick have each been invaluable for their assistance and encouragement. I thank everyone in my family, especially my brother Peter.